I0814815

INSIDE MLB

DETROIT TIGERS

Sam Rhodes

www.av2books.com

Go to **www.av2books.com**, and enter this book's unique code.

BOOK CODE

AVE32333

AV² by Weigl brings you media enhanced books that support active learning.

AV² provides enriched content that supplements and complements this book. Weigl's AV² books strive to create inspired learning and engage young minds in a total learning experience.

Your AV² Media Enhanced books come alive with...

Audio
Listen to sections of the book read aloud.

Video
Watch informative video clips.

Embedded Weblinks
Gain additional information for research.

Try This!
Complete activities and hands-on experiments.

Key Words
Study vocabulary, and complete a matching word activity.

Quizzes
Test your knowledge.

Slide Show
View images and captions, and prepare a presentation.

... and much, much more!

Published by AV² by Weigl
350 5th Avenue, 59th Floor
New York, NY 10118
Website: www.av2books.com

Library of Congress Control Number: 2017963687

ISBN 978-1-4896-7974-1 (hardcover)
ISBN 978-1-4896-7975-8 (softcover)
ISBN 978-1-4896-7976-5 (multi-user eBook)

Printed in the United States of America in Brainerd, Minnesota
1 2 3 4 5 6 7 8 9 0 22 21 20 19 18

012018
120817

Project Coordinator: John Willis   Designer: Nick Newton

The publisher acknowledges Getty Images, Alamy, and iStock as its primary image suppliers for this title.

Contents

During their long history, the **Tigers** have sent a total of **22 players** to the **Baseball Hall of Fame.**

GO, TIGERS!

Detroit, Michigan, is a city known for its automotive industry, its music, and its professional sports. Fans are especially proud of their baseball team, the Detroit Tigers. The team has a rich history. Some of the best players in baseball have worn the navy blue, orange, and white of the Tigers. There is much to learn about this unique team.

In 2017, Nicholas Castellanos, with help from first base coach Omar Vizquel, became the sixth Tiger in history to score 25 home runs, 100 runs batted in, and 10 triples in a single season.

With help from slugger Miguel Cabrera, the Tigers finished first in their division four times between 2011 and 2014.

Who Are the Tigers?

The Detroit Tigers play in the Central **Division** of the American League (AL). Major League Baseball (MLB) is divided into the American League and the National League (NL). Both leagues have three divisions: East, Central, and West. The best team in each division, plus two **wild card** teams, makes the **playoffs**. The Tigers have made the playoffs 16 times since 1901. They have won four **World Series** championships.

Considered one of the best players in the history of baseball, outfielder Ty Cobb held many records when he retired. However, he never won a World Series championship.

WHERE THEY CAME FROM

The Detroit Tigers became a major league team in 1901. They were called the Tigers from the first day they took the field, and Detroit has been their home for all of their 117 seasons. In their first nine years as a team, they went to three World Series championships. They lost all three, but went on to have many outstanding seasons.

Second baseman Ian Kinsler was one of the AL's top 10 players for hits during the 2014, 2015, and 2016 seasons.

Who They Play

Every season, the Detroit Tigers play 162 games. They play against each of the other teams in their division 19 times. That is a total of 76 division games every season. The other teams in their division are the Chicago White Sox, the Minnesota Twins, the Kansas City Royals, and the Cleveland Indians. The Cleveland Indians are the Tigers' biggest **rivals**. Fans love to watch these two teams compete against each other.

Where They Play

The Tigers play home games in Detroit's Comerica Park. Comerica Park opened in the summer of 2000. It took three years to build, but was worth the wait. Inside the park, there is a Ferris wheel, a carousel, and a museum. The park can seat more than 41,000 fans at a time. Before Comerica Park, the team played in Tiger Stadium for 39 years.

The baseball field inside Comerica Park sits 25 feet (7.6 meters) below street level. Fans without tickets can watch games from the street.

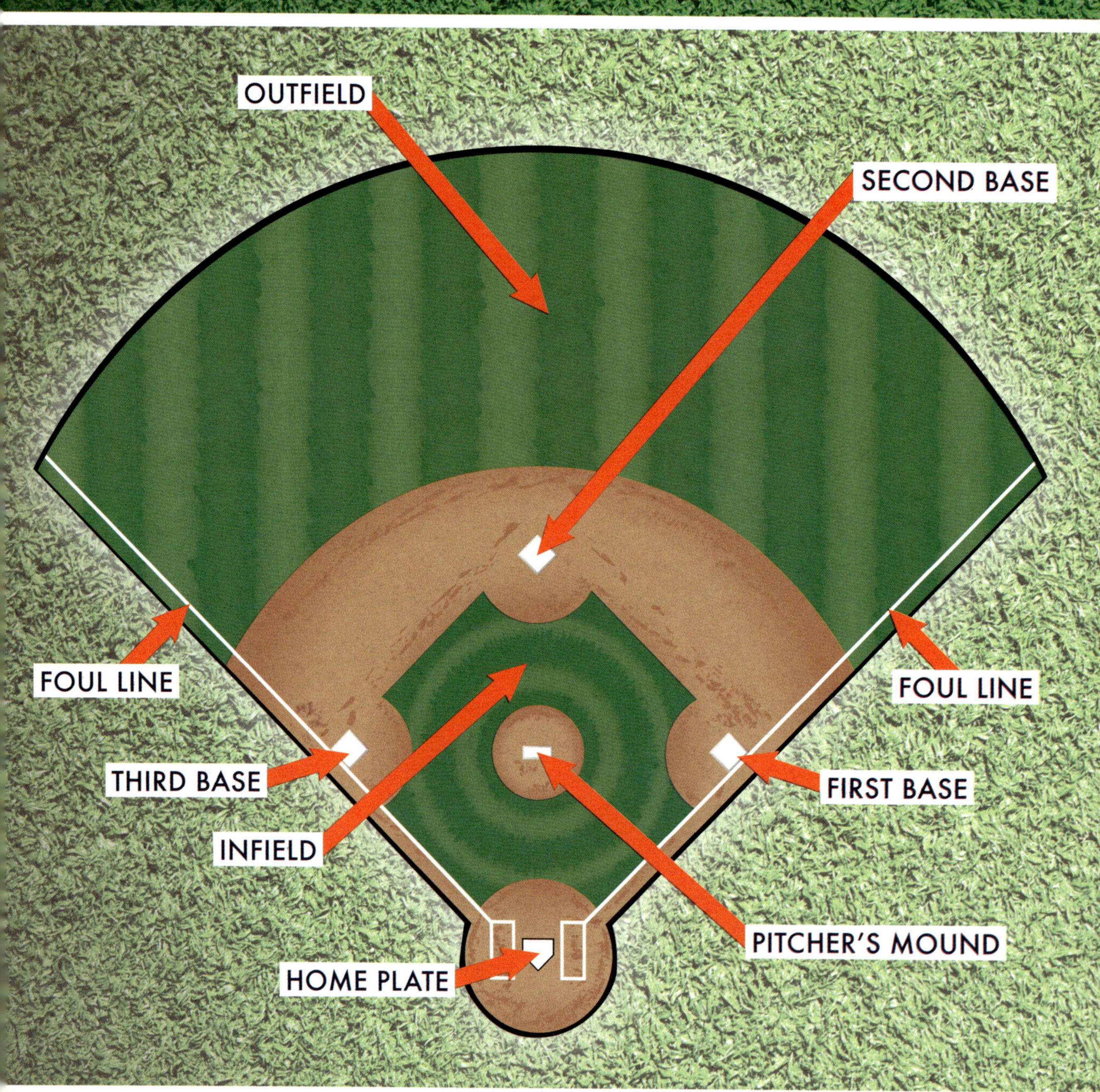
OUTFIELD
SECOND BASE
FOUL LINE
FOUL LINE
THIRD BASE
FIRST BASE
INFIELD
PITCHER'S MOUND
HOME PLATE

THE BASEBALL DIAMOND

Baseball games are played on a field called a diamond. Four bases form this diamond shape. The bases are 90 feet (27 m) apart. The area around and between the bases is called the infield. At the center of the infield is the pitcher's mound. The grass area beyond the bases is called the outfield. White lines start at **home plate** and go toward the outfield. These are the foul lines. Baseballs hit outside these lines are out of play unless a fielder catches them. The outfield walls are about 300–450 feet (91–137 m) from home plate.

Big Days

Over their 117-year history, the Tigers have had some exceptional seasons. Here are some of their finest:

1935: *The Tigers were determined to make it to the World Series after their fourth failed attempt in 1934. In 1935, they played the Chicago Cubs for the championship. In Game 6, they made out with a 4–2 victory. They claimed their first World Series win.*

1984: *The Tigers finished the season with a dominant 104–58 record. Winning four straight games, they claimed the American League* ***Pennant****. They then clobbered the San Diego Padres in the World Series, winning four games to one. From the season opener to the World Series win, they stayed in first place.*

2012: *For most of the 2012 season, the Tigers struggled. Then, in September, they pulled together and won their division. On a roll, they swept the New York Yankees and took the AL Championship.*

During the 2012 season, the Tigers won 70 percent of games led by pitcher Max Scherzer.

Although considered a shoe-in for the Hall of Fame, first baseman Miguel Cabrera had a rough 2017 season due to injuries.

Tough Days

The Tigers have seen many ups and downs. Here are a few of their toughest moments:

1915: *After several disappointing years, 1915 looked promising. The Tigers finished a strong season with 100 wins. Unfortunately, the Boston Red Sox finished with 101 wins, just edging the Tigers out of the postseason.*

1940: *Detroit finished first in their league. In the World Series, they faced the Cincinnati Reds. Led by pitcher Bobo Newsom, the Tigers won the first game easily. Going into Game 6, they led the series 3–2. One more win would clinch it. Buckling under the pressure, they lost the next two games and the championship.*

2017: *After coming close to a World Championship five years earlier, the Tigers tried to regain momentum. However, they found themselves finishing last in their division. Winning less than 40 percent of their games, it was their worst season in more than 10 years.*

MEET THE FANS

Through good times and bad, fans of the Detroit Tigers remain steadfast. Every year, thousands of people pour into Comerica Park to root for the home team. Some fans even paint their faces like tigers to show their support. Paws, the team's mascot, does not have to paint his face. He already looks just like a tiger! Born in 1995, Paws likes collecting baseball cards and playing with friends.

In 2016, Paws helped celebrate the 11th annual ¡Fiesta Tigres! by wearing a special jersey. This event celebrates the contributions of Latino baseball players and coaches.

Denny McLain, Pitcher

With the Tigers, Ty Cobb's batting average was .368. This means he hit 36.8 percent of the times he was at bat.

Heroes Then...

The Tigers **franchise** has featured many star players throughout the years. Center fielder Ty Cobb played with Detroit from 1905 to 1926. To this day, he has the best career batting average of any player in the history of baseball. Hal Newhouser was one of the Tigers' best pitchers. He won back-to-back **Most Valuable Player (MVP)** awards in 1944 and 1945. Pitcher Denny McLain led the Tigers to the 1968 World Series. He also won the **Cy Young Award** and the MVP award in the American League that year. Right fielder Al Kaline's incredible batting helped the Tigers win the 1968 World Series. Lou Whitaker was Rookie of the Year when he started for the Tigers in 1977. In his 19 years with the team, Whitaker earned five consecutive **All-Star Game** picks from 1983 to 1987. As one of the best second basemen in baseball, he earned the **Gold Glove Award** in 1983, 1984, and 1985.

Heroes Now...

The Detroit **roster** is packed with spectacular players. Nicholas Castellanos is a strong hitter, leading the American League in triples. Seven-time **Silver Slugger Award** winner Miguel Cabrera is a talented hitter. Michael Fulmer was Rookie of the Year in 2016 as a pitcher. In the 2017 All-Star Game, he represented the Tigers. With continued hard work and a little luck, he will have a long and decorated career. Second baseman Ian Kinsler is a veteran on the team. Kinsler joined four American League All-Star teams between 2008 and 2014. These Detroit Tigers are heroes on and off the field. Autographs for a Cause is a charitable program offering signed copies of baseball cards in return for a donation. The player then matches that donation and all the money goes to charity. Through these kinds of programs, the Detroit Tigers are giving back to their community.

The present-day Tigers are loaded with star players.

GEARING UP

Baseball players all wear a team jersey and pants. They have to wear a team hat in the field and a helmet when batting. Take a look at Alex Avila and Ian Kinsler to see some other parts of a baseball player's uniform.

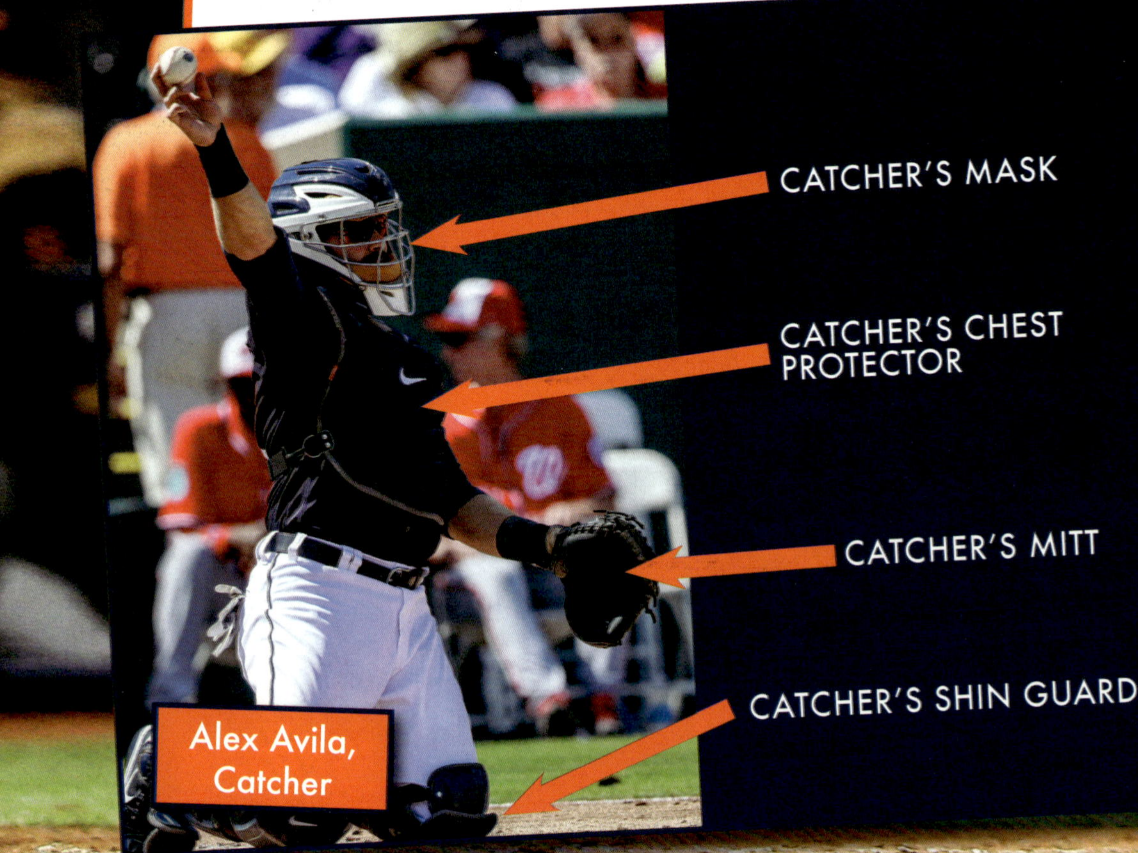

Alex Avila, Catcher

Ian Kinsler,
Second Baseman

SPORTS STATS

Here are some all-time career records for the Detroit Tigers. All of the stats are through the 2017 season.

A Major League baseball weighs about **5 ounces** (142 grams). It is **9 inches** (23 centimeters) around. A leather cover surrounds **hundreds** of feet of string. That string is wound around a small center of **rubber** and **cork**.

Home Runs

Al Kaline, **399**

Norm Cash, **373**

Runs Batted In

Ty Cobb, **1,811**

Al Kaline, **1,582**

Batting Average
Ty Cobb, **.368**
Harry Heilmann, **.342**

Stolen Bases
Ty Cobb, **869**
Donie Bush, **402**

Wins by a Pitcher
Hooks Dauss, **223**
George Mullin, **209**

Wins by a Manager
Sparky Anderson, **1,331**
Hughie Jennings, **1,131**

Earned Run Average
Harry Coveleski, **2.34**
Ed Killian, **2.38**

Quiz

1 How many Tigers players are in the Hall of Fame?

2 How many times have the Tigers made the playoffs?

3 How many World Series championships have the Tigers won?

4 In what year did the Detroit Tigers become a major league team?

5 Who are the Tigers' biggest rivals?

6 Where do the Tigers play home games?

7 What is the name of the Tigers' mascot?

8 Who has the best career batting average of any player in history?

Answers

1. 22
2. 16
3. Four
4. 1901
5. The Cleveland Indians
6. Comerica Park
7. Paws
8. Ty Cobb

Key Words

All-Star Game: an annual midseason game in which the best players from the AL and NL play against each other

Cy Young Award: an annual award given to the best pitcher in each league

division: a group of teams that forms one part of a professional sports league

franchise: a team that belongs to a professional sports league

Gold Glove Award: an annual award given to a player from each defensive position in each league

home plate: the base where a batter stands that a runner must touch to score a run

Most Valuable Player (MVP): an annual award given to one player from each league

pennant: a commemorative flag given to the champions of each league

playoffs: the additional games played after the regular season to determine an overall champion

rivals: teams that have a strong sense of competition with each other

roster: a list of players on a team

Silver Slugger Award: an annual award given to a player from each offensive position of each league

wild card: a team, other than the top teams, that also qualifies for the playoffs

World Series: an annual series played between the champions of each league

Index

Log on to www.av2books.com

AV² by Weigl brings you media enhanced books that support active learning. Go to www.av2books.com, and enter the special code found on page 2 of this book. You will gain access to enriched and enhanced content that supplements and complements this book. Content includes video, audio, weblinks, quizzes, a slide show, and activities.

AV² Online Navigation

Audio
Listen to sections of the book read aloud.

Book Pages
AV² pages directly correspond to pages in the book.

Video
Watch informative video clips.

Embedded Weblinks
Gain additional information for research.

Key Words
Study vocabulary, and complete a matching word activity.

Try This!
Complete activities and hands-on experiments.

Quizzes
Test your knowledge.

Slide Show
View images and captions, and prepare a presentation.

AV² was built to bridge the gap between print and digital. We encourage you to tell us what you like and what you want to see in the future.

Sign up to be an AV² Ambassador at www.av2books.com/ambassador.

Due to the dynamic nature of the Internet, some of the URLs and activities provided as part of AV² by Weigl may have changed or ceased to exist. AV² by Weigl accepts no responsibility for any such changes. All media enhanced books are regularly monitored to update addresses and sites in a timely manner. Contact AV² by Weigl at 1-866-649-3445 or av2books@weigl.com with any questions, comments, or feedback.